PUT ON A MAGIC SHOW
AND OTHER GREAT LEGO® IDEAS

Pick an activity...

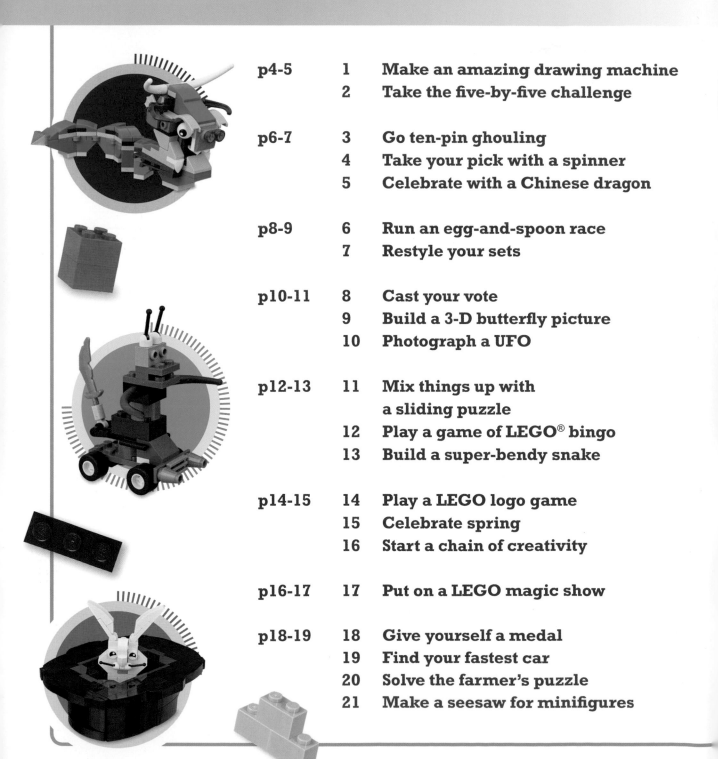

1 Make an amazing drawing machine

You can make all kinds of patterns with this magnificent machine – all you have to do is turn the handle! The gear wheels move the pen and the paper, and swirling shapes begin to appear before your eyes!

Experiment with different gear combinations – what happens when a big gear turns a small gear?

Use a marker for the best results

Turn this handle to work the mechanism

These grey beams move the pen in an oval shape

Pins with ball ends stop the rubber band from coming off

The drawing board must have a smooth tiled surface

Panels make sides for the drawing board

Four plates with pins underneath connect a large gear wheel to the bottom of the drawing board

The drawing board turns on this pin

Two rubber bands hold a square of paper in place

A rubber band pulls these two beams together to hold the pen

Pins and angle beams hold the frame together

CHANGING GEAR

The machine works because the gear wheels move the pen in one direction, while the drawing board turns the other way. Using different combinations of gears, or changing where the pen arm connects to, would create a different pattern. Try overlaying different patterns on the same piece of paper, using different-coloured pens.

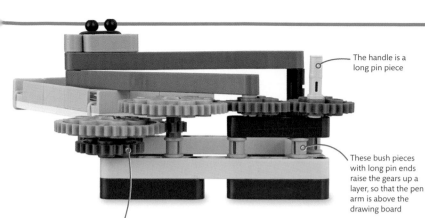

The handle is a long pin piece

These bush pieces with long pin ends raise the gears up a layer, so that the pen arm is above the drawing board

Stacking two gears on one axle allows the sequence of gears to move down a layer

BACK TO THE DRAWING BOARD

When you have mastered the mechanics of the drawing machine, you could develop the idea with a bigger drawing board, or by adapting the pen arm to hold two pens at once. However you choose to make your patterns, keep them and use them to make gift tags and greeting cards.

BUILDER'S TIP

A complicated LEGO® Technic build like this can be even more fun if you let a grown-up join in to help you with perfecting the functions.

Take the five-by-five challenge

2

Grab five lots of five different types of brick, then see what you can build using all 25 bricks in five minutes! These models are made using five 1x1 round plates, five 1x1 bricks, five 1x2 bricks, five 2x3 bricks and five 2x4 bricks.

Don't worry about what colour the bricks are

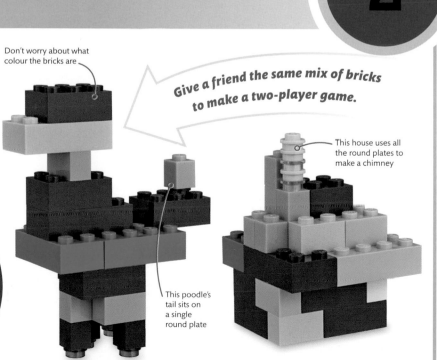

Give a friend the same mix of bricks to make a two-player game.

This house uses all the round plates to make a chimney

This poodle's tail sits on a single round plate

BUILDER'S TIP

Don't be afraid to change your build into something else halfway through. Five minutes is a long time!

3 Go ten-pin ghouling

Ten-pin ghouling is just like ten-pin bowling, only spookier! A ghostly figure lurks at the end of this dark alley, and the pins are a gang of scary creatures. Try not to shake as you roll the ball, and aim for a strike – if you dare!

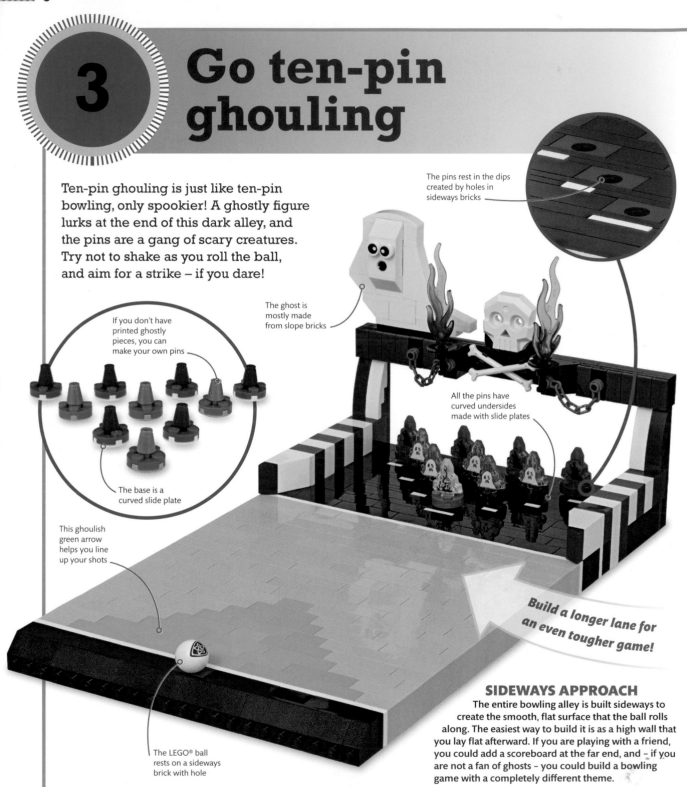

The pins rest in the dips created by holes in sideways bricks

The ghost is mostly made from slope bricks

If you don't have printed ghostly pieces, you can make your own pins

The base is a curved slide plate

All the pins have curved undersides made with slide plates

This ghoulish green arrow helps you line up your shots

Build a longer lane for an even tougher game!

The LEGO® ball rests on a sideways brick with hole

SIDEWAYS APPROACH
The entire bowling alley is built sideways to create the smooth, flat surface that the ball rolls along. The easiest way to build it is as a high wall that you lay flat afterward. If you are playing with a friend, you could add a scoreboard at the far end, and – if you are not a fan of ghosts – you could build a bowling game with a completely different theme.

Take your pick with a spinner

4

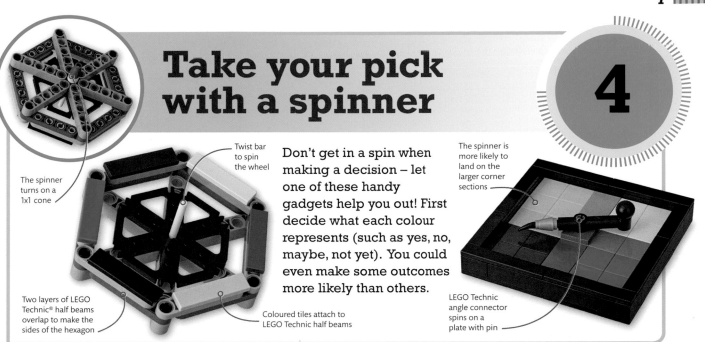

The spinner turns on a 1x1 cone

Twist bar to spin the wheel

The spinner is more likely to land on the larger corner sections

Don't get in a spin when making a decision – let one of these handy gadgets help you out! First decide what each colour represents (such as yes, no, maybe, not yet). You could even make some outcomes more likely than others.

Two layers of LEGO Technic® half beams overlap to make the sides of the hexagon

Coloured tiles attach to LEGO Technic half beams

LEGO Technic angle connector spins on a plate with pin

Celebrate with a Chinese dragon

5

In China, people see in the New Year and other important events by dancing with life-size dragon puppets. Mark a special occasion of your own by building a miniature dragon.

The dragon's back is made with curved slopes

Eyebrows are made from wheel arch pieces

Horns slot into plates with side rings

Frilly crest is made from minifigure flippers!

Bottom half is made from slope bricks

Each section is linked to the next with hinge plates

6 Run an egg-and-spoon race

See how far you can run before your LEGO egg falls from the LEGO spoon! Build two eggs and spoons for a race, or take turns to see who can run the furthest.

Just two studs hold the top and bottom of the egg together

Add a yolk and white inside your egg

Hold the handle part of the spoon only

DO YOU WANT BACON WITH THAT?

Overlap long plates to make a sturdy spoon handle

End of the spoon is a large radar dish

What would the LEGO® Friends Heartlake Food Market look like if it was a LEGO® Pirates set? Maybe something like this! Using the instructions for one of your sets as a starting point, see if you can build it as if it belonged to a different play theme, with different colours and fun details.

BUILDER'S TIP

Plan ahead! Think about what kinds of themed pieces you have before you start building.

The upper level is a jail, rather than a pretty apartment

THE SAME, BUT DIFFERENT

This pirate blacksmith shop is the same size and shape as the Friends set it is based on, but it looks completely different. What would a LEGO® NINJAGO® fire station look like? Or a LEGO Friends spaceship?

BACK

Pirates prefer plain benches to pink ones!

Food for sale, just like at the Friends market

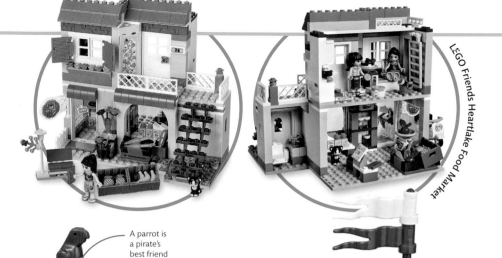

LEGO Friends Heartlake Food Market

7

Restyle your sets

A parrot is
a pirate's
best friend

FRONT

A robot arm and
a shield make an
old-fashioned sign

They don't dress
like this in
Heartlake City!

Defensive spikes
replace flowers
at this window

Heavy wooden
door instead of a
modern glass one

Base plate is the
same size as in
the Friends set,
but in an earthy
tan colour

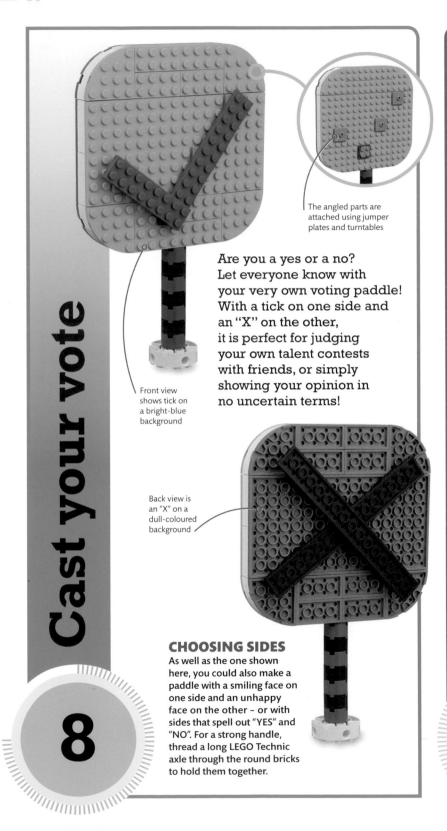

Cast your vote

The angled parts are attached using jumper plates and turntables

Are you a yes or a no? Let everyone know with your very own voting paddle! With a tick on one side and an "X" on the other, it is perfect for judging your own talent contests with friends, or simply showing your opinion in no uncertain terms!

Front view shows tick on a bright-blue background

Back view is an "X" on a dull-coloured background

CHOOSING SIDES

As well as the one shown here, you could also make a paddle with a smiling face on one side and an unhappy face on the other – or with sides that spell out "YES" and "NO". For a strong handle, thread a long LEGO Technic axle through the round bricks to hold them together.

8

Create the butterfly first, then build the white background around it

SPREAD YOUR WINGS

Start by building the middle part of the butterfly from round bricks, and add plates coming out in two directions to form an "L" shape. Each wing should look like a mirror image of the other, and both are built in the same way – just at different angles.

This wing is made more realistic by having one section slightly higher than the other

A frame makes the build look more like a work of art

9

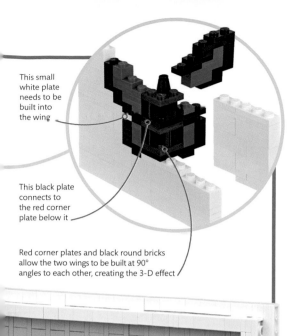

This small white plate needs to be built into the wing

This black plate connects to the red corner plate below it

Red corner plates and black round bricks allow the two wings to be built at 90° angles to each other, creating the 3-D effect

Photograph a UFO

10

Amaze your friends with photos of unidentified flying objects soaring through the sky! Use a transparent antenna or bar to hold a micro-scale model in front of your camera.

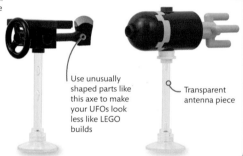

Dome pieces make a hot-air balloon shape

Transparent radar dish piece

Use unusually shaped parts like this axe to make your UFOs look less like LEGO builds

Transparent antenna piece

Blue bricks make it look like this butterfly is flying in a clear blue sky

Wow! These butterflies really fly out at you! They would be great builds all by themselves, but by building them into a larger flat background they look like pictures that have come to life. Be sure to show yours off before it flies away!

Build a 3-D butterfly picture

11 Mix things up with a sliding puzzle

When does a pattern become a puzzle? When you split it up into sliding shapes! Each part of this design is made from a plate that moves on hidden grooves and rails, so that you can mix it up and make a game. Time yourself to see how long it takes to put the pattern back together again!

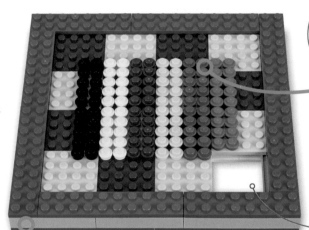

Each puzzle piece has two rails created by overhanging jumper plates

There are grooves along the opposite sides, which the other pieces slot into

Each piece slots into the pieces above and to the left, or into the outer frame

Leave one free square so that the puzzle pieces can move around

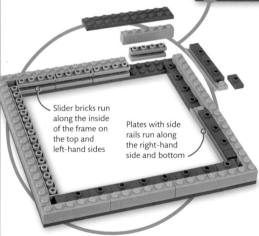

Slider bricks run along the inside of the frame on the top and left-hand sides

Plates with side rails run along the right-hand side and bottom

PIECING IT ALL TOGETHER

Start by building 12 puzzle pieces, but don't decorate the tops yet. Slot the 12 puzzle pieces into the frame in three columns, and then build three more puzzle pieces inside the frame. When all 15 puzzle pieces are in, decorate the tops with round plates. Scramble the pieces to create the puzzle! Make sure you take a photo of the completed puzzle first or refer to this page when putting the pattern back together again.

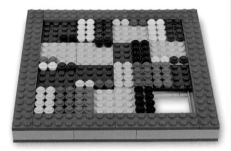

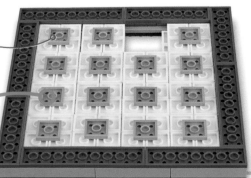

The bottom of each puzzle piece is held together with a 2x2 plate

Four 2x2 jumper plates are sandwiched between another layer of jumper plates and a 4x4 plate

THE SPECIAL BRICK

Slider bricks have a groove along one side so that rails or tiles can slot into them and move from side to side. They can be used to make moving platforms and sliding doors.

12 Play a game of LEGO® bingo

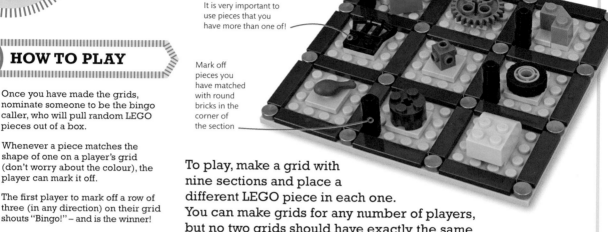

It is very important to use pieces that you have more than one of!

Mark off pieces you have matched with round bricks in the corner of the section

HOW TO PLAY

1. Once you have made the grids, nominate someone to be the bingo caller, who will pull random LEGO pieces out of a box.

2. Whenever a piece matches the shape of one on a player's grid (don't worry about the colour), the player can mark it off.

3. The first player to mark off a row of three (in any direction) on their grid shouts "Bingo!" – and is the winner!

To play, make a grid with nine sections and place a different LEGO piece in each one. You can make grids for any number of players, but no two grids should have exactly the same bricks. Who will be the first to shout "Bingo!"?

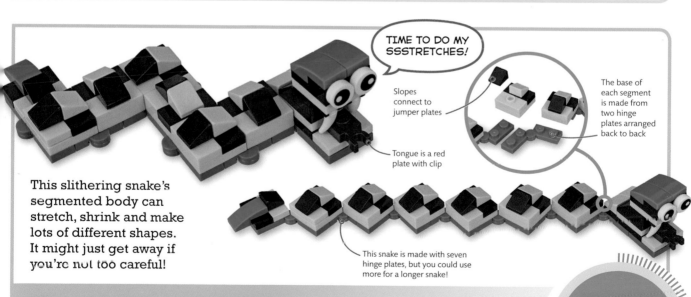

TIME TO DO MY SSSTRETCHES!

Slopes connect to jumper plates

The base of each segment is made from two hinge plates arranged back to back

Tongue is a red plate with clip

This slithering snake's segmented body can stretch, shrink and make lots of different shapes. It might just get away if you're not too careful!

This snake is made with seven hinge plates, but you could use more for a longer snake!

Build a super-bendy snake

13

14 Play a LEGO logo game

The world is full of logos – on storefronts, billboards and even LEGO sets! See how many logos you can build from LEGO bricks, and then quiz your friends to see which ones they can name.

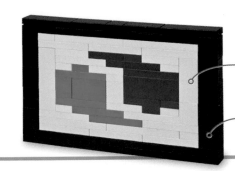

This LEGO Exploriens logo (a 1990s LEGO Space® subtheme) is built flat using plates

The Octan logo has been used in LEGO® Town and City sets since 1992

This logo is built upright, using layers of bricks and plates

15 Celebrate spring

The cute bunny ears are slope bricks mounted on single bricks

Both arms are half arch bricks

The carrot is built around a plate with a ring that looks like a clutching paw

Slope bricks make wide bunny cheeks

Fluffy tail is a large flower

Spring is a lovely time of year. When it comes around, why not make some LEGO models to mark the occasion? If it seems a long way off, you can build something that reminds you of it! The rabbit, chick and egg are all symbols of spring. How would you represent it?

Each leg connects to a LEGO Technic pin with an axle end

LEGO Technic pin sits inside 1x6 brick with holes

Start a chain of creativity

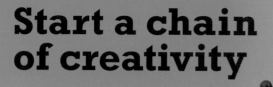

The first 10 pieces make a simple car

The next player adds another 10 pieces that they grab from the pile!

Player three sees how the horns could become arms and adds a head and tail

16

HOW TO PLAY

1 Sit around a big pile of LEGO bricks with your friends. Set a timer to 1 minute. Each player selects 10 bricks and starts to build.

2 After 1 minute, each player passes their model to the player on their left. Reset the timer to 1 minute. Each player adds another 10 pieces to the model now in front of them.

3 Repeat steps 1–2 until eveyone has added bricks to all the models. Admire the bizarre models you have created!

Can you be creative under pressure? Play a timed building game with your friends and find out. Watch as your models get stranger and stranger!

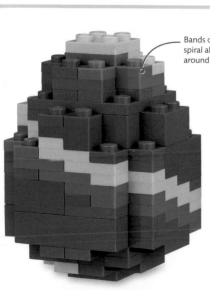

Bands of colour spiral all the way around the egg

Offset slope looks like messy feathers

Both feet are a single plate

Wings are slope bricks

SIGNS OF SPRING
Other springtime builds could involve flowers and blossom, lambs, new green leaves, blue skies and sunshine. But the most important thing is what the season means to you, so be imaginative – all year round!

THE SPECIAL BRICK

The mini antenna piece can be used for all kinds of things – whiskers, insect antennae, weapons, arms and more!

17 Put on a LEGO magic show

Come one! Come all! See a minifigure disappear before your very eyes! Gasp as rabbits are pulled from a hat! Question everything you thought possible as a pizza is shrunk to the size of a coin! Ladies and gentlemen, boys and girls, see all this and more with your very own LEGO magic models!

Doors have grey plates with side rails at the tops and bottoms, which allow the doors to slide open and shut

Dazzling stars distract the eye

THE SPECIAL BRICK

Plates with side rails are perfect for making sliding doors. The rails slide along bricks with a groove.

MINIFIGURE MAGIC

Make a minifigure disappear! You'll need to build a magician's cabinet with closing doors and a revolving wall. The minifigure stands on a platform attached to the revolving wall. When the wall is turned, an identical platform is revealed – but there is no minifigure! A successful magic trick is all about distracting the eye, so make sure your cabinet is as colourful and creative as possible, and remember to wave your magic wand with one hand as you turn the revolving wall with the other!

Ta da! When the doors open the minifigure has disappeared!

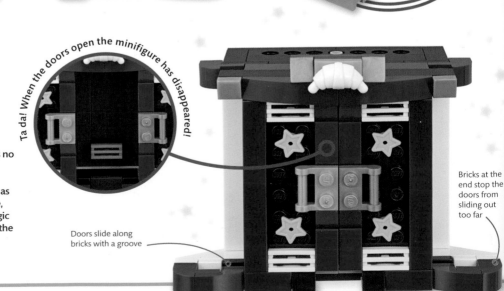

Bricks at the end stop the doors from sliding out too far

Doors slide along bricks with a groove

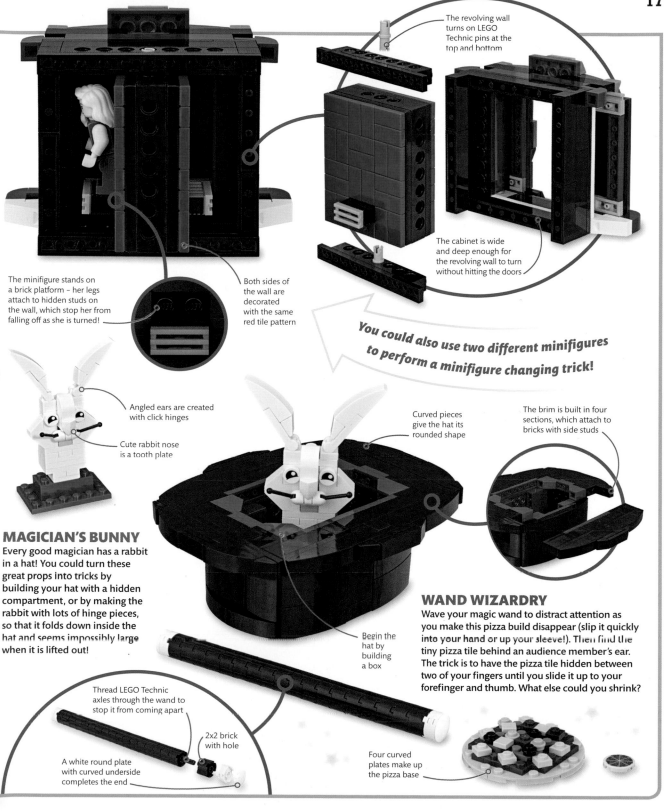

The revolving wall turns on LEGO Technic pins at the top and bottom

The cabinet is wide and deep enough for the revolving wall to turn without hitting the doors

The minifigure stands on a brick platform – her legs attach to hidden studs on the wall, which stop her from falling off as she is turned!

Both sides of the wall are decorated with the same red tile pattern

You could also use two different minifigures to perform a minifigure changing trick!

Angled ears are created with click hinges

Cute rabbit nose is a tooth plate

Curved pieces give the hat its rounded shape

The brim is built in four sections, which attach to bricks with side studs

MAGICIAN'S BUNNY

Every good magician has a rabbit in a hat! You could turn these great props into tricks by building your hat with a hidden compartment, or by making the rabbit with lots of hinge pieces, so that it folds down inside the hat and seems impossibly large when it is lifted out!

Begin the hat by building a box

WAND WIZARDRY

Wave your magic wand to distract attention as you make this pizza build disappear (slip it quickly into your hand or up your sleeve!). Then find the tiny pizza tile behind an audience member's ear. The trick is to have the pizza tile hidden between two of your fingers until you slide it up to your forefinger and thumb. What else could you shrink?

Thread LEGO Technic axles through the wand to stop it from coming apart

2x2 brick with hole

A white round plate with curved underside completes the end

Four curved plates make up the pizza base

18 Give yourself a medal

Do you know someone who deserves a medal? Maybe it's you! Make first, second and third place medals and award them for the games in this book.

Use two layers of round plates to create the numbers

You could thread a ribbon through this curved plate with hole

19

RAMP IT UP

One way to build a racing ramp is to link together LEGO base plates and prop them up with a shallow stack of books. If the studs slow things down too much, turn the base plates upside down. Don't make the ramp too steep, or the cars will simply fall off it.

Small front wheels for extra speed

Here is a puzzle to build, solve – and then set for your friends! A farmer needs to get a fox, chickens and some grain across a river – but he only has room in his boat for himself and one of those three things! He will have to make several trips, but he knows that if he leaves the chickens behind with the grain, they will eat it – and if he leaves the fox with the chickens, it will eat them! In what order will he get everything across?

Both arms are built sideways and connect to a 1x2 brick with four side studs

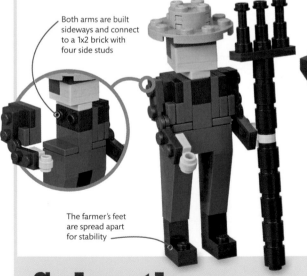

Chickens are built around small bricks with four side studs

The farmer's feet are spread apart for stability

The fox's back is made from curved plates

Solve the farmer's puzzle

You can find the solution on page 32 ▶

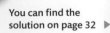

Find your fastest car

I'M GOING DOWNHILL FAST!

Large back wheels for grip

Every race car needs a driver

What's the fastest LEGO car in your collection? Find out by running two cars down a slope and seeing which one reaches the finish line first! Pit the winner against another car and keep adapting your builds – or build a new car – until you find a car that no other can match!

Try all the wheels and tyres you have to find the fastest combination.

A slim car will slice through the air with ease, but if it is too thin it will tip over!

The wheels are attached to a plate before the car body is added

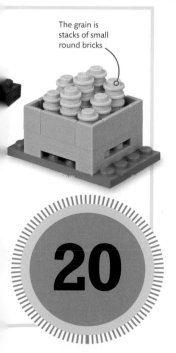

The grain is stacks of small round bricks

20

The minifigures add equal weight at both ends

Hinge cylinder pieces hold the two sides at the same angle

The seesaw balances on a LEGO Technic pin with ball connector

The base is a large radar dish

These two minifigures rock back and forth on one tiny ball, but they don't tip over! Can you add more or different pieces and still make the seesaw swing?

21

Make a seesaw for minifigures

22 Create a friendly gnome

THERE'S GNOME PLACE LIKE HOME!

Hat is made from rocket and nose cone pieces

Spectacles are transparent round tiles

Hoe for cutting weeds

Toadstool cap is a construction worker's helmet

Lance makes a perfect fishing rod

Feel like giving a gnome a home? This gnome will look great watching over your pot plants or window boxes. Gnomes are friendly, but they can get up to mischief, so don't leave them outside or you might find they wander off!

Play football with straws

23

Challenge your friends with this scaled-down football game. Two players each have a straw, which they use to try to get the ball into their opponent's LEGO goal – just by blowing!

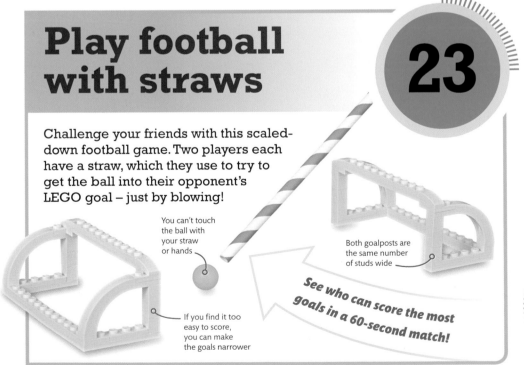

You can't touch the ball with your straw or hands

Both goalposts are the same number of studs wide

If you find it too easy to score, you can make the goals narrower

See who can score the most goals in a 60-second match!

MAKE IT SNAPPY
The build is really one big hinge, linked by LEGO Technic pins at the back of the head. The two halves of the mouth are built separately, and then connected by the pins. Add a long brick coming out of the back of the top half – when you push down on it, the shark's jaws will open wide!

24

KNOW YOUR GNOMES

Most gnomes are short and plump, with pointy hats, beards and brightly coloured outfits. They like to help out in the garden, so they often carry shovels or push wheelbarrows. If there is water nearby, they also enjoy some fishing. What will your gnome be doing?

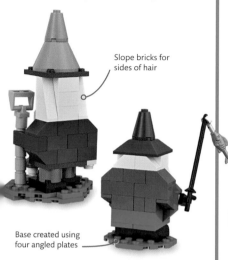

Slope bricks for sides of hair

Base created using four angled plates

Why not make different racks for different kinds of video games?

Put your video game collection in order with a LEGO rack for your game cases. Place what you're playing at the front, so you can see its stylish cover art.

The cases rest on smooth tiles

This rack has room for three video game cases

Add a decoration – this musical note shows that this rack is for dance and karaoke-style games

25 Organise your games

Build a shark with bite

Press here to open

LEGO Technic pins connect the two halves of the mouth

Curved pieces add a smooth finish above and below the teeth

The teeth sections fit sideways onto angle plates at the front and sides of the mouth

Don't be scared by this great white shark – all it eats is paper clips! Press the lever at the back and its mouth opens wide. Reach inside and claim the clips you need before its shiny white jaws snap shut again!

THE SPECIAL BRICK

1x1 tooth plates aren't just for making teeth! They can also look like ice, claws, noses, beaks and much more!

26 Give a LEGO greetings card

Show someone how much you care with a greetings card to mark a special occasion – or just to say hello! These cards aren't for sending in the post, so you get to give them in person. You could also leave one on display, so the lucky person you made it for gets a surprise!

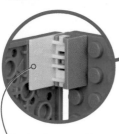

Both cards open on hinge bricks at the top, middle and bottom

Bright, colourful decorations will make your card stand out

You will need two large plates the same size to make your card.

A message is spelled out with LEGO plates inside

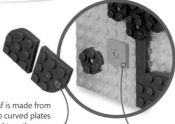

Leaf is made from two curved plates held together by a round plate

The round plate attaches to a jumper plate, connecting the leaf to the card

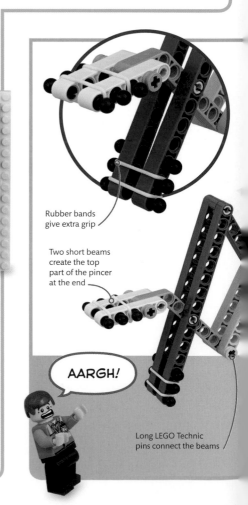

Rubber bands give extra grip

Two short beams create the top part of the pincer at the end

AARGH!

Long LEGO Technic pins connect the beams

BUILDER'S TIP

You could also build a card from the bottom up using bricks instead of plates, with hinge plates to connect the two sides.

A CARD FOR ANY OCCASION

As well as birthday cards and season's greetings, you could also make get well messages, thank you cards and cards that congratulate people on passing school tests or getting new jobs. Make the picture on the front reflect the kind of card that you are making, or add the favourite things of the person that you are making it for.

27

Put your memory to the test

Use pieces that are easy to name, such as a skateboard or snake

Take on your friends with this tricky memory challenge! Spread 20 or 30 pieces out on a table and ask all the players to study them for one minute, then cover them up. Next, everyone has two minutes to write down as many pieces as they can remember. Whoever lists the most correct pieces is the winner!

Here is a great way to keep your room neat without having to break a sweat! Grasping the end of this extending arm makes it reach out for almost 30 inches (76cm), grabbing onto whatever it finds in its path. Nothing can escape its clutches!

This pin must be placed off-centre for the handle to work

Squeeze the top and bottom handle beams to extend the arm

PLACING THE PINS

All six yellow LEGO Technic beams and the three dark-grey beams are connected by long LEGO Technic pins at both ends and in their very center. However, the middle pins in the blue and red beams are offset from the centre to create the pincer at the front and the handle at the back.

Use more LEGO Technic beams to make your grabber even longer!

Make a long-armed grabber

28

29 Keep yourself cool

Smooth tile decorations stop sections from getting stuck to each other when the fan is folded in

Tile is on top section only

THIS TRULY IS MY BIGGEST FAN.

Wall panel pieces below each hinge stop the sections from opening out too far

Hinge plates link each section

Each section is a long angled plate

Hand fans have been used throughout history to keep people cool and help them look cool, too! What colours and pieces will you use to decorate your folding LEGO fan?

30 Put together some percussion

Make some noise with these builds! Make a shaker by placing loose small bricks inside a simple container. To expand your band, add a rain stick – a tall tower with loose pieces that sound like falling rain when they knock against the hidden obstacles inside.

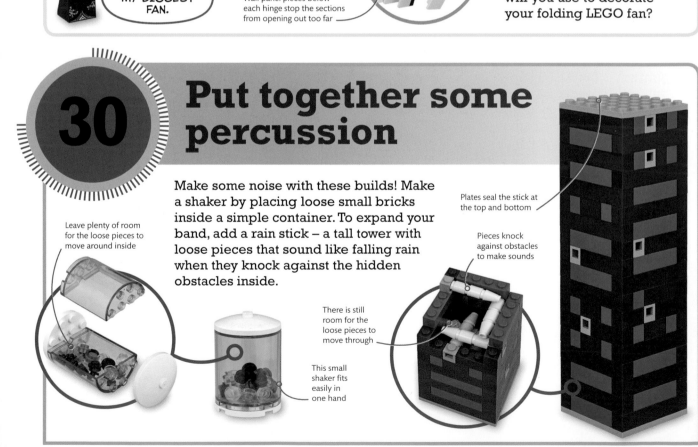

Leave plenty of room for the loose pieces to move around inside

There is still room for the loose pieces to move through

This small shaker fits easily in one hand

Plates seal the stick at the top and bottom

Pieces knock against obstacles to make sounds

Build a paper aeroplane launcher

31

Give your paper aeroplanes an extra boost with a smooth runway and a flick-firing launch mechanism made from LEGO Technic pieces. Use a small piece of paper to make an aeroplane and then take turns with a friend using the launcher and see who can make their plane fly the furthest.

Watch your paper aeroplane soar through the sky!

Two grille slopes support the plane before launch

Flick here to send your plane up, up and away!

When released, the lever pushes the aeroplane up from the bottom

Long LEGO Technic pin limits the movement of the beam

The plane sits loosely within this channel

Tyres attach to long LEGO Technic pin

Use your launcher to test your best paper aeroplane designs.

The lever is a LEGO Technic beam that fits onto an axle

The axle slots into a brick with a cross hole, which is built into the stand

LIFT-OFF LEVER
The firing mechanism is a lever that pivots on a LEGO Technic axle in the base of the launcher. The lever's length adds to its power, while the tyres make it easier to flick and give it extra momentum when it is in motion.

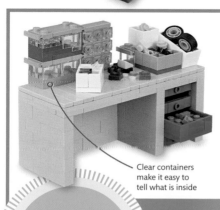

Clear containers make it easy to tell what is inside

32

Sort your LEGO bricks

Sorting your bricks by size and type can make building even more fun because you can find the parts more quickly and easily. Collect small plastic tubs to store all your different parts. Try organising parts by shape first. Sorting by colour can make finding things harder – imagine trying to find a particular yellow piece in a box full of yellow pieces!

Brick-drop challenge

Test your nerves in this exciting two-player game! Inside the brick-drop tower are lots of loose LEGO pieces, supported by sticks made from LEGO Technic axles. Players take turns removing the sticks – and then watch as the loose pieces take a tumble!

LEGO Technic axles overlap to create a lattice to hold the pieces

HOW TO PLAY

1 Place all the sticks in the tower, then pour a handful of small pieces into the top.

2 Each player sits in front of one of the two trays. Take turns removing a stick from the tower – gently!

3 As sticks are removed, the bricks will start to fall and land in the trays. Peek through the sides of the tower to guess which way you think the pieces will fall.

4 When all the sticks have been removed, the winner is the player with the fewest pieces in their tray.

Transparent rock bricks let players see inside the tower

Layers of bricks with holes allow sticks to cross through the model

Pieces on the end of the sticks stop them from sliding through the model

Lid rests on a layer of smooth tiles

Ornate pillars are decorative – but not essential!

Slope bricks help hold the tower clear of the base

33

Tiles stop the tray from sliding on the base

Tray is a square wall element

Add the bricks with holes at different levels on alternate sides.

FROM TOP TO BOTTOM

The brick-drop tower is hollow and open at both ends so that the loose pieces can be added, and can then fall through to the trays below. The trays slot neatly into place between decorative tiles on the base, but do not attach to anything. They are easy to remove so that you can pour the loose pieces back into the top and play again!

34 Build a pair of bookend buddies

Ears are grill slopes

Layers of curved plates surround the eyes

The tail is made from a mixture of angled plates

BEING A BOOKEND IS A REAL HOOT!

This friendly fox and wise old owl are great pals. They never let anything come between them – unless it's a good book! They spend their days back to back, guarding all the knowledge and excitement that is found on a bookshelf, and making any room much more colourful!

The owl's feathery front is created with croissant pieces

The backs of the bookends are completely flat

Make sure your bookend can support one or two books before adding more

BALANCING THE BOOKS

Both animals are built sideways from a base of thin plates using curved and angled bricks to make a simple outline. Make sure the bookends are deep enough not to tip over. Adding bricks all through the insides, rather than having hollow space, also gives them the solid weight they need to support real books.

Key details are created with a top layer of plates

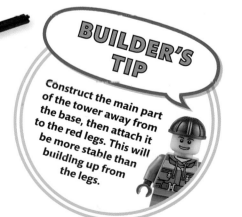

BUILDER'S TIP

Construct the main part of the tower away from the base, then attach it to the red legs. This will be more stable than building up from the legs.

Challenge your friends and family with a pair of near-identical LEGO scenes and see if they can spot the differences against the clock! Ten things have changed in each of these scenes. Can you identify them all in three minutes? Try to build your own pair of scenes, too. Remember to include lots of small details!

Spot the difference

1

Keep key pieces, like this blue base plate, the same in both builds

LEGO Technic connectors create a curvy tree trunk

1

Build in lots of opportunities to add detail, like this brick with clip

Hide differences inside compartments for an extra challenge!

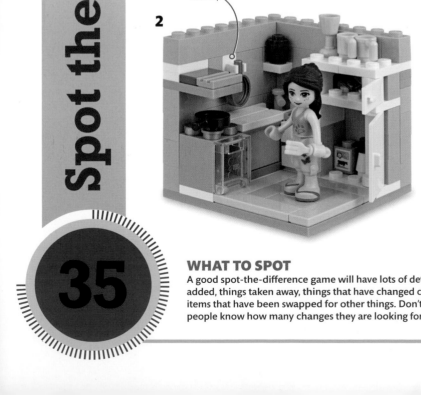

2

2

35

WHAT TO SPOT

A good spot-the-difference game will have lots of detail, with things added, things taken away, things that have changed colour, and items that have been swapped for other things. Don't forget to let people know how many changes they are looking for!

Find the full list of differences for each model on page 31 ▶

36 Take aim in tin alley

Bring all the fun of the fairground into your own home with this classic tin target game. Take turns with your friends seeing how many tins you can knock down, or try to hit them all in 30 seconds.

The launcher can swivel from side to side on this turntable

Look through this LEGO® BIONICLE® sight to take aim

Turn the cogs to tilt the launcher up and down

Use this handle to aim the launcher left and right

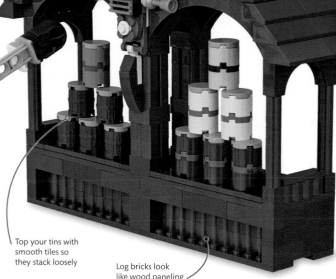

Top your tins with smooth tiles so they stack loosely

Log bricks look like wood paneling

Move the launcher closer or further away to make the challenge easier or tougher

FAIREST OF THEM ALL

Fancy stalls in carnival colours add to the excitement of funfair games. Make your tin can alley stall as appealing as the real thing by adding decoration and detail all over.

Tall round bricks look like wooden poles

THE SPECIAL BRICK

This chunky housing has a spring-release mechanism that fires a missile when the lever at the back is pulled.

37 Keep the kitchen clean

Create a build that's not only bright and attractive, but really useful, too! This practical paper towel dispenser is a quick and convenient way to keep your kitchen neat, and the LEGO frame itself is easy to clean with a little warm water.

Thinner end sections slot into the sides

A single-stud connection makes it easy to change the roll

Eight layers of long overlapping plates make a strong rail

DISPENSING ADVICE

Build your dispenser with a rail that slots into the sides from above, rather than sitting on top of them. That way, it will lift out easily when you want to change the roll, but won't come off when the towels are pulled forward. Build it with a broad base, so that it doesn't tip over when pulled.

You could use colours to match the decor in your kitchen

Make sure your build is tall enough to hold a full roll of towels

OOPS! I SPILLED MILK AGAIN!

BUILDER'S TIP

Measure the length of a roll of towels before you build – your rail should be slightly longer than the roll.

Pull a building idea out of a hat

38

Someone came up with an idea to build a lobster!

LOOK WHAT I BUILT!

I'M RUNNING OUT OF TIME!

Have a random selection of bricks on hand

Play a game that is great for getting ideas and sharing inspiration with your friends! Ask players to write five building ideas on pieces of paper and fold them up. Place them in a bag and get everyone to select one at random – without showing it to the other players. Give everyone five minutes to build the idea they picked. When the time is up, see if you can all guess what everyone has built!

39

Try a pair of calipers for size

Make a tool that will help you get the measure of your LEGO bricks! These calipers will tell you how many plates it takes to span any brick, which is especially useful for sideways building.

Build the moving part separately and slide it on from the bottom.

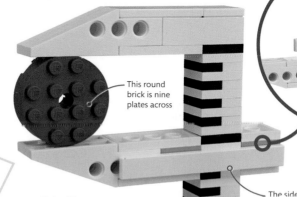

This round brick is nine plates across

Bricks with side studs hold the tiles in place

The sides of the moving part are long tiles

Units of five are marked with a bigger black plate

DK Penguin Random House

Senior Editor Helen Murray
Senior Cover Designer Mark Penfound
Senior Designers Jo Connor, David McDonald, Anthony Limerick
Editors Pamela Afram, Beth Davies, David Fentiman, Laura Palosuo, Natalie Edwards, Matt Jones, Helen Leech, Clare Millar, Rosie Peet
Designers Ellie Boultwood, Rhys Thomas, Thelma Jane-Robb, Gema Salamanca, Abi Wright
Pre-Production Producer Kavita Varma
Senior Producer Kathleen McNally
Managing Editor Paula Regan
Design Managers Jo Connor, Guy Harvey
Creative Manager Sarah Harland
Publisher Julie Ferris
Art Director Lisa Lanzarini
Publishing Director Simon Beecroft

Models built by Joshua Berry, Jason Briscoe, Stuart Crawshaw, Naomi Farr, Alice Finch, Rod Gillies, Kevin Hall, Barney Main and Drew Maughan
Photography by Gary Ombler

Dorling Kindersley would like to thank Randi Sørensen, Paul Hansford, Martin Leighton Lindhardt, Henk van der Does, Lisbeth Finnemann Skrumsager, Michael Madsen and Jens Rasmussen at the LEGO Group. Thanks also to Julia March at DK for editorial assistance and Sam Bartlett for design assistance.

First published in Great Britain in 2017 by
Dorling Kindersley Limited 80 Strand, London, WC2R 0RL

Contains content previously published in *365 Things to do with LEGO® Bricks* (2016)

001-310865-Oct/17

Page design copyright © 2017 Dorling Kindersley Limited.
A Penguin Random House Company.

LEGO, the LEGO logo, the Minifigure and the Brick and Knob configurations are trademarks of the LEGO Group. All rights reserved. © 2017 The LEGO Group. Manufactured by Dorling Kindersley, 80 Strand, London, WC2R 0RL, under licence from the LEGO Group.

A CIP catalogue record for this book is available from the British Library.

ISBN: 978-0-2413-3067-8

Printed in China.

www.dk.com
www.LEGO.com

A WORLD OF IDEAS:
SEE ALL THERE IS TO KNOW

Solutions

20 SOLVE THE FARMER'S PUZZLE
P18–19

• The farmer and the chickens cross the river (the fox and grain are safe together). He leaves the chickens on the opposite side of the river and goes back across to the fox and grain.

• The farmer then takes the fox across the river, but because he can't leave the fox and chickens together, he brings the chickens back.

• Again, because the chickens and grain can't be left together, he leaves the chickens and he takes the grain across and leaves it with the fox.

• He then returns to pick up the chickens and heads across the river one last time.

35 SPOT THE DIFFERENCE P29

① Different-coloured walls
② Frying pan missing from wall
③ Different pan on cooker
④ Different-coloured cupboard door
⑤ Different-coloured floor pattern

① Different bird in tree
② Missing brickwork detail behind tree
③ Different windowpane design
④ Pirate has different-coloured pants
⑤ Different-coloured chest

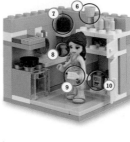

⑥ Goblet added to row of mugs
⑦ Different-coloured can in corner
⑧ Different-coloured faucet
⑨ Different utensil in mini-doll's hand
⑩ Different carton in bottom of fridge

⑥ Different-coloured flag
⑦ Fewer leaves on tree
⑧ Different item in pirate's hand
⑨ Extra barrel behind tree
⑩ Different treasure in chest

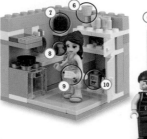